EXIT STRATEGY

ALEX CARTER, CFP,® CIM®

EXIT $TRATEGY

A GUIDE TO SUCCESSFULLY SELLING YOUR BUSINESS

LIONCREST
PUBLISHING

EXIT STRATEGY

A Guide to Successfully Selling Your Business

FIRST EDITION

ISBN   978-1-5445-3102-1 *Hardcover*
   978-1-5445-3101-4 *Paperback*
   978-1-5445-3103-8 *Ebook*

To my father, Rudi, thank you for leading, teaching, and believing in me.

To my mother, Ellie, thank you for always loving, supporting, and guiding me.

To my wife, Haelie, you are the best partner and most supportive person I could have in my life. Thank you for your continued love and optimism.

To my children, Rylie and Hudson, thank you for all the love you bring into my life.

CONTENTS

INTRODUCTION

Are you a successful business owner who has spent years—or even decades—building a company from humble beginnings to a profitable and prominent presence? If so, congratulations on a fantastic achievement! You've likely invested substantial monetary and sweat equity. Additionally, you've probably generated numerous well-paying jobs and influenced the world with your creation.

Whether your business is related to retail, manufacturing, software, or anything else, there comes a time when you reflect on how your professional life has developed and what your future holds. You might start to think about leaving the company you've created and grown for so long. As the ancient proverb suggests, "All good things must come to an end."

Fortunately, the "good thing" you've established is almost certainly worth a lot of money. The end of your involvement should translate to a wonderful opportunity for you to do whatever is next. Perhaps it involves starting or acquiring another business? Maybe it's focused on philanthropy or volunteerism? It could be as worthwhile and straightforward as spending more time with friends and family. Perhaps it's something else, or even a combination of a few things? With the abundance of financial resources you stand to receive from selling your business, the options are limitless.

With that in mind, ask yourself: "Is it time to exit my business?"

If you suspect the answer might be yes to that question, you've come to the right place.

As someone who has bought and sold businesses and developed a network of esteemed professionals to help others do the same thing, I would like to help you develop an exit strategy to enable whatever you want to do next in your life.

KICKSTART YOUR EXIT PLAN

Another old saying states, "When you fail to plan, you plan to fail." After reading this book, the planning won't be a problem. You'll be prepared for everything an exit strategy requires. Better yet, you'll be equipped to walk away from your business financially secure, emotionally healthy, and ready for whatever comes next.

When considering the sale of your business, it's natural for a swirl of emotions to consume your headspace; fear, doubt, and anxiety might be chief among them. Amidst those feelings is a spectrum of questions to which you need answers. Who will be your buyer? How do you prepare the business for sale? What dollar figure should you have in mind? Will the business thrive without you? Will you thrive without it?

To put an end to the uncertainty in your mind, you need to kickstart your plan a little earlier than you might realize.

Whatever your reasons and goals are for exiting your business, you need to start planning at least three to five years before you officially want to walk away.

With that in mind, a stark truth remains: most business owners don't have an exit plan at all. They're far too busy running the day-to-day operations of their business to think about how someday they'll leave it. After all, a business owner's to-do list is lengthy whether running a new business, a growing successful business, a mature business (where early retirement is possible), or considering late retirement. These are the natural evolutionary phases that a business owner goes through, and it helps to understand where you're at, regardless of how strongly you're thinking about selling.

NEW BUSINESS

PLAN BUSINESS STRUCTURE → CREATE SAVINGS GOALS
Amounts and locations (RRSPs, corporation, TFSAs, non-reg) → INITIAL ESTATE PLAN → TAX OPTIMIZE PORTFOLIO

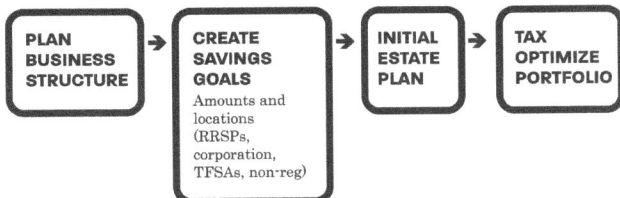

GROWING SUCCESSFUL BUSINESS

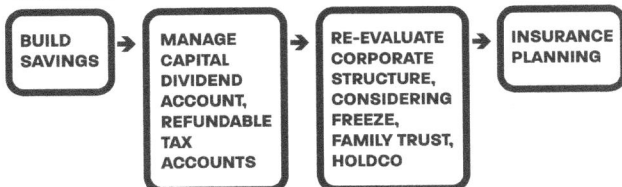

BUILD SAVINGS → MANAGE CAPITAL DIVIDEND ACCOUNT, REFUNDABLE TAX ACCOUNTS → RE-EVALUATE CORPORATE STRUCTURE, CONSIDERING FREEZE, FAMILY TRUST, HOLDCO → INSURANCE PLANNING

MATURE BUSINESS/EARLY RETIREMENT

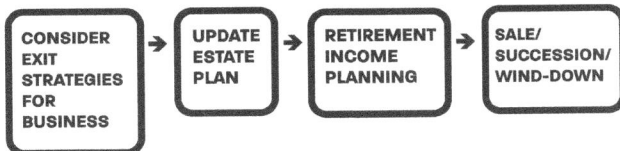

CONSIDER EXIT STRATEGIES FOR BUSINESS → UPDATE ESTATE PLAN → RETIREMENT INCOME PLANNING → SALE/ SUCCESSION/ WIND-DOWN

LATE RETIREMENT

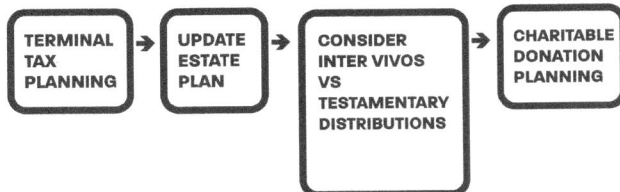

TERMINAL TAX PLANNING → UPDATE ESTATE PLAN → CONSIDER INTER VIVOS VS TESTAMENTARY DISTRIBUTIONS → CHARITABLE DONATION PLANNING

I've spoken with countless business owners over the years. Some have sold for tens of millions of dollars; others for much less. The commonality is that they're all extremely busy people who don't have the time to take on an exit strategy as a solo endeavour. That's OK, because selling a business is not a simple task meant to be tackled by any individual; it is a complex process that requires a team effort.

Soon you'll discover how to build your exit team of professionals who can take care of all the details while ensuring you get top dollar to hand over your life's work to a competent successor. With the right team in place, you won't need to worry about the information overflow that can bring chaos into a solo effort.

Rest assured, however, that this book will not detail the convoluted minutiae involved in the lengthy and complex process of a successful exit strategy. That's what your exit team is for. You won't see an abundance of graphs, charts, and textbook-style reference material to memorize and reiterate when appropriate. This book will *not* include industry-specific jargon related to tax laws or legalese. You also won't see an overly complicated process about executing any particularly tedious task, negotiating contracts, or navigating buyer-seller engagements.

Rather, simple storytelling with strategies and tips will summarize my numerous exchanges over the years with business owners and expert colleagues who have experience collaborating on successful exit strategies. I've also conducted numerous interviews specifically to answer questions that anyone looking to exit a business would want to know. These carefully curated pieces of information will serve as peace of mind that you're doing the right thing and you're doing it the right way.

By the end of our journey, you'll know how to kickstart your plan and emerge from your sale wealthy, healthy, happy, and wise. Notice how the first of those feelings is the only one that pertains to a financial outcome. The last three are aspects of your physical and mental well-being. Don't overlook the importance of these concerns when leaving your business.

Now that you know what this book is and what it isn't, you need to know who I am, what I do, and why I'm uniquely suited to express my thoughts and recommendations for helping to build your exit strategy.

A WEALTH ADVISOR AND EXIT STRATEGY TEAM MEMBER

My name is Alex Carter, and I have successfully bought and sold multiple businesses—the first of which I purchased from my father in 2011, and it has since grown to five times its original purchase price value.

Today I am the branch owner of multiple Assante Capital Management Ltd. locations. One site is in Toronto, Ontario and the other is in Collingwood, Ontario. In those areas, I serve as a senior wealth advisor for over 150 successful families and business owners. In 2019, I was awarded the organization's top overall ranking for advisors under forty years old.

In addition to finance and entrepreneurship, I have a deep-rooted passion for philanthropy. My father and I created a family foundation where we've coordinated charitable events across Canada for over ten years. We continue giving back to our community by helping the underprivileged through charities like the Salvation Army (and many others) and by contributing to the preservation of the Bruce Trail in Ontario, among other areas of conservation land.

Through a wonderful program called Vision 2020, I have also set up my own foundation to help build knowledge for young philanthropists in Toronto. Additionally, I work on the board of a nonprofit and run the finance committee of another. As you can probably tell, philanthropy and volunteerism are a big part of my life, and I'm comforted to know that I'm not in the minority of business owners in that regard. Many of my clients and colleagues also have philanthropic goals they want to achieve.

When selling a business, people often want to know how they can continue to maximize their charitable contributions to the causes they care about most. I'm always careful to consider this desire and other unique goals for my clients.

As a wealth advisor, I am well-equipped to serve as a valuable member of your exit team. Of course, if you're not near one of my branches, or if you choose to use the services offered by another financial strategist, you can still benefit from the ideas presented in this book.

THREE OPTIONS FOR SELLING YOUR BUSINESS

Now that you know a little about me and how I can help, you should know about the three options for potential buyers who will come to you.

- **Family**—Many business owners wish to hand down their life's work to one of their children as a legacy manoeuvre. Watching your business being capably run by a son or daughter can be an especially rewarding experience.
- **Employee**—Some business owners know of an employee who is particularly well-suited and interested in purchasing their business. Handing the keys over to an exceptional employee can provide peace of mind in knowing that your business is in capable hands to survive and thrive beyond your involvement.
- **External Third Party**—Oftentimes, a third party will express interest in your business if it seems to be a good fit for their portfolio. This is a scenario where an excellent mergers and

acquisitions (M&A) lawyer might be necessary, depending on the valuation of your business and the complexity of the transaction.

Nuances exist in each of these options, but one thing remains crucial: the necessity to assemble a highly skilled and qualified team. Keep that theme of team building in mind, because it will ease the burden of thinking you have to know every detail of all the tasks, laws, and regulations that happen in the sale of your business. You don't. By simply choosing your team members wisely, you'll reap the rewards of a successful transaction executed one small step at a time.

ONE SMALL STEP AT A TIME

The first step toward forming your exit strategy is to read a quick summary of how the sale of a business *can* happen. In the next section, I'll provide a summary with key takeaways of what happened when my father sold his business to me. This anecdote provides a good precedent for anyone considering selling their business to a family member. This section will also provide essential information related to the other seller options.

From there, I will dive into how to build your exit team of expert professionals. As mentioned previously, this is a crucial concept. It is likely the most important aspect of building an effective exit strategy.

After that, a section regarding what to do/not do will give you awareness of key aspects to be particularly mindful of during the process. In the final section, you'll read several stories of what an exit strategy looks like from the perspective of business owners who have successfully navigated the process. Professionals with varied expertise will also share valuable insight to ensure you get the best results possible.

This book will then conclude with a recap of what you've learned and a to-do checklist to serve as handy reference material throughout your sale. Resist the urge to skip ahead to the conclusion, as the wrap-up isn't effective without the detail provided throughout the book.

The information that follows will be an easy read and provide an invaluable resource for forming an exit strategy without regret. Once you follow through on these recommendations and implement your plan, a new world of possibilities for life after your business will be made available to you. Enjoy the journey!

THE THREE TYPES OF BUYERS FOR YOUR BUSINESS

Different business owners are looking for different outcomes when selling their businesses. Ask yourself what the most important factor is for you to consider your sale a successful one.

You might be looking to maximize value and walk away from the business with little or zero care for what happens to it after you're gone. That's fine. A business owner's motive for selling is a judgment free zone. In this situation, finding a buyer is a fairly simple task. Seek the highest bidder and take it from there.

On the other hand, many business owners feel like they have built something they care about on a deeper level. Maybe you've taken a great deal of pride in watching your business grow and give back to the community. If you've been in business for twenty, thirty years or more, you've developed an extensive client base. When you serve clients well for that many years, they may become friends; they also create referrals that help to scale your business. In that case, finding a buyer is a bit more of a complex process because you won't want to sell your business to just anybody. You'll want to make sure the clients who put their trust in you for all those years remain in good hands. That means searching for a buyer who is good with people, enabling a culture match not only with your clients, but also with your existing management team. Furthermore, you'll want to ensure the buyer has satisfactory experience and knowledge of the industry, as well as a proven track record of success. If you can find a buyer that meets those criteria, you'll sleep better at night, knowing that you did right by the people who helped to shape your success as a businessperson.

Perhaps your intentions—like many business owners—lie somewhere in the middle. This happens when you care to know that the business and its people will thrive after you're gone, but you're not willing to give away too much in the sale price to make sure it happens.

Whatever your reason for selling is, you need to find the right buyer to fulfill your vision of a successful exit strategy.

Selling your business can be a complex process, regardless of who the buyer is. Let's start our exploration of your options with a personal anecdote about how my father sold his business to me. If you have a child or someone else in your family whom you think would be a suitable successor, by reading our story, you'll know what you might expect from a family-based transaction. After that, you'll read about the other two types of transactions—employee-based and third-party.

WHAT TO KNOW ABOUT A FAMILY-BASED SALE

Business owners are typically successful because of their relationships with clients. A rapport must be established with the clients that builds trust. Clients are everything to a business. Therefore, if the long-term well-being of your company is a factor in determining a successor for your business, you must find someone who is great at fostering relationships with clients. That trust you built must pass from your hands to theirs. This becomes a much easier task if you're selling to a family member or employee because they likely have an existing relationship with the clients and are familiar with their needs. That was the case when my father handed his business over to me, and I think it can serve as precedent for other family-based or employee-based sales.

I began working at the head office of Assante through a university program in the summer of 2003. Becoming a financial advisor and business owner was always something I thought about, but it wasn't my first plan for the future.

Although my father and I had always discussed my potential in his business on a more permanent basis, I initially planned to be a sports medicine doctor. Sports have always been a passion of mine. Squash, in particular, is my game.

You could say I "had my cake and ate it too," because

I pursued my passion for sports by playing first division NCAA for squash, but still chose the business route for my career. Upon graduation from the University of Western Ontario in 2006, my father convinced me to work at his branch of Assante Capital Management Ltd. in Toronto.

It didn't take much convincing. As early as fourteen years old, I had frequently approached my father with the idea that someday I could take over the family business. Once I finally joined, my long-term goals were clear: I wanted to be a business owner. So my father knew that this was on my radar as soon as I onboarded.

Something similar might be happening in your business. Is there a family member who seems well-suited to take over? If there is, have a discussion with them. You'll want to cover a few things: First, you want to know if they want to take over. Then, you want to find out if they're capable of actually doing it. Third, you want to talk about how and when you can make that happen.

My dad and I started talking about how we would transition the business to me in 2007. That's when his exit strategy began. I need to give my dad a lot of credit here. He didn't just ask me to take over one day and hand me a contract the next. He spent time in an invaluable mentorship period first while getting all the other pieces in place.

Slowly, he began to bring me into more meetings of greater importance. I started to see things from beyond the role of the individual as he showed me the big picture of how the organization ran. By understanding more of the inner workings of his business, I started to learn how everything comes together.

That same year, my wife and I moved only three blocks from my dad in Toronto. That living situation made it possible for us to carpool to work and have daily conversations about the business. Those drives to work became part of an accelerated education in being a business owner.

It's hard to get that level of mentoring unless you're extremely close to the person. If you're considering a family or employee-based transaction, find a way to spend extra time with them talking about the business. If you can carpool together, great. If not, maybe you can have lunch together a couple of times a week. Perhaps you can enjoy a daily thirty-minute walk outside of the office while talking business. Think creatively and you'll come up with something. The information you share during those times can add up to a lot of knowledge-based value in the long run.

Previously, I mentioned how exit strategies take more time than most people think. Three years is possible, but it's still a bit rushed. It would be doable but difficult to educate someone, even a close family member, on all the details of the business in this time frame. Five years is much more ideal. With five years as a transition period, you'll have time (just like my father and I did) to get deep into the nuts and bolts of the business's operations.

Our transition time coincided with the global economic crisis of 2008-2009. While this was a horrible time for the industry and investors, it was timely for me to watch how my father managed the situation. It was so helpful for me to notice how he navigated this uniquely challenging event in our global economy. I don't think I could have gotten that experience anywhere else—not in any classroom or any other job.

In 2011, I officially took over the leadership of his business. The funny thing is I have two siblings, which means my father had options on whom to transition the business to. Any of us would have served the company well, and he had full knowledge of that. This means I had no leverage in negotiations.

My father's concern wasn't about money. It was much more about being careful not to display any favoritism. He gave each of us a fair chance at acquiring the business. My only recourse (if I wanted the company badly enough, and I did) was to pay more than the full asking price, which amounted to an offer of several million dollars.

Throughout the process, my father got outstanding tax and legal advice. He leaned heavily on his CPA and lawyer because he had developed a good relationship with them. One of the best pieces of advice he got was to sell a large portion of the business as goodwill. That simple act created significant tax advantages, which his CPA was wise to recommend.

His lawyer then ensured the deal was a simple and fair purchase and sale. That's a big advantage of selling to a family member. The contract doesn't necessarily need to include complex terms to protect either party. Of course, outliers exist in anything, so some family transactions may not be quite as cut and dry.

After the papers were signed and my ownership became official, my father stuck around for about a year. He didn't show up in anything close to his previous capacity, but he was there to ensure a smooth transition. One day he realized that everything was running smoother than ever, and he just stopped showing up.

I was fortunate that my father already had an exemplary group of people working for him, so there was no need to change that. I retained all the existing staff. By working closely with your prospective buyer, you can showcase the skills of the people you already have on your current team. Not only does this provide peace of mind in job security for your staff, but you'll be adding value to the sale by handing over a competent set of personnel with the transaction.

The benefits of our transaction were evident for

both of us. It was a family-based sale from father to son, so no sneaky side deals were happening. And I took over a profitable business with a proven track record of growth with a capable staff.

For me, the deal worked out beyond expectations. Although I had to pay top dollar for the business, I have grown it substantially. Today my branches have a significant presence in the industry, and we're doing great things with our success. Not only do we provide high-paying jobs to a lot of great performers, but we also give a lot back to the community by donating our time and money to worthy causes. I made those promises before I bought the business, and I'm happy to say that I've followed through with them.

From my father's perspective, he knew the business he built from scratch was in good hands. He also knew that the people who worked so hard for him for so long would have jobs. My father felt comforted and reassured, knowing that the clients who became good friends and helped him to grow his business, would continue to be well served going forward. There was also peace of mind for him in knowing his son was in control of his destiny while being able to make an earnest living. Overall, my father appreciated the benefits of a well-organized exit strategy in many ways:

- He sold for top dollar, which allowed him to contribute a sizable portion of the profit from the sale to goodwill and extend his philanthropic goals into retirement.
- By selling to his son, he enhanced his legacy. The business he built from scratch has lived on within the family and thrives beyond his day-to-day involvement.
- My father recognized retirement for the opportunity it is. He spends a lot of time with his grandchildren. He's also physically active, working out almost every day, hiking, skiing, golfing, and playing squash.
- Walking away from his branch office has given him time to manage the many properties he owns.

It's easy to see how firmly my dad has embraced his post-business life. Because there were no surprises during the sale and he planned nearly five years ahead of his desired "walk away day," he retired with no regrets. He is happy, healthy, more than financially secure, and enjoying an active but low-stress retirement lifestyle. If any of this sounds like something you want, you can do this too.

The key to a successful exit strategy, regardless of whom you're selling to, is and always will be proper planning.

WHAT TO KNOW ABOUT AN EMPLOYEE SALE

In the deal with my father, I grew the business and he got to enjoy his retirement to the fullest. Such mutual benefit can also happen when selling to an employee. Whether you're selling to a family member or an employee, your first question (unless you truly don't care what happens to the business or the people in it after you leave) should always be, "Is this person capable of running this business after I leave?" When selling to an employee, you'll want to ask yourself some additional questions:

- Is the employee capable of coming up with enough money to buy the business?
- Are they using traditional financing through a bank?
- Is seller-based financing an option that would help the buyer and that you would consider?

- Are they hoping to buy just a portion of the business? If so, is increasing their ownership incrementally over time an option you would both consider? This could be executed in a way that allows the employee to slowly assume more responsibilities until they either have majority ownership or can buy you out completely.
- How are you planning on bringing the employee into ownership? If the employee leaves, this can get messy unless you have a shareholder agreement in place. You can also provide them percentages of your business through equity ownership or stock options.

Employee and third-party buyers tend to be cautious when taking over a company without the founder's influence going forward. They almost certainly don't understand the business the way the founder does. Many times, they'll ask for a gradual rollover of ownership. In this situation, the founder might stay on for up to eighteen months, showing the new owners how the business operates inside and out. After that, the buyer usually feels comfortable enough to take over without the founder coming in on a regular basis. At some point, they'll want to firmly take control anyway. If a gradual rollover is the chosen method of transition, the buyer and seller need to work out the terms of how long the founder will stay on to show them the ropes and how they'll be compensated for their consultancy.

Another good way to handle the transition of operation is through consultancy, which is a trend I see more often in business acquisitions. The seller walks away from the business without any required transition period. Instead, they collect a consulting fee for their services when helping the buyer learn specific key processes or nuances of the industry. For the buyer, consultancy can work out especially well because the founder no longer influences the corporate culture by being there every day. The buyer gets to put their stamp on the business while still getting expertise from the person who knows how things work better than anyone else.

If you're considering selling your business to an employee, they're probably a great performer and fully capable of running it. They're also most likely a trusted member of your inner circle of relationships. You'll also achieve the satisfaction of knowing that you've given someone close to you a highly valuable asset. In those ways, the employee-based transaction is similar to the family-based sale. The third-party sale, however, is a bit different.

WHAT TO KNOW ABOUT A THIRD-PARTY SALE

Whereas family-based transactions and employee sales are executed under mostly amicable conditions, the third-party sale can get a little more complicated. After all, you're most likely familiar with a family member or an employee to whom you're selling the business, but the third party is likely to be someone you know little to nothing about, at least in the beginning.

A third-party transaction is often referred to as an "arm's length transaction." In this type of deal, neither party is influencing the other. Both parties are operating independently and should have equal access to all information related to the agreement.

Another key difference with a third-party sale is that a more rigorous due diligence process is required. Whereas a family member or a high-level, trusted employee may have intimate knowledge of the inner workings of the business, a third party would likely know little to nothing beyond what they see in the media, on a website, or elsewhere.

The origin of most third-party sales may surprise you. Many business owners I've spoken with have told me they expected to hire a firm to find the best buyer but were pleasantly surprised when someone from their own network expressed interest.

When looking for a third-party sale, buyers often come from your own network. Often, a colleague or someone else who is close to the business steps in if they have a clue that you might be willing to sell. An offer like this could come from almost anywhere; it could even come from a competitor looking to buy you out. This reinforces the notion of "never burning a bridge" in your business relationships.

Keep your interactions with colleagues amicable. Someday one of those people who think highly of you may be the right person to take over the business when you're ready to leave. Even if you're not looking to sell for a long time, this act of positive professionalism may pay off in the long run.

The third-party transaction is also where you need

to be especially careful not to just sign a contract without proper legal representation reading it and interpreting it sufficiently.

I've seen deals where one party lost value by signing an agreement without legal assistance. Good legal advice is incredibly important for anybody considering the sale of their business.

The old saying is "buyer beware," but in an exit strategy, it's also a good idea to think "seller beware."

THINK BIG PICTURE

The information regarding the types of sales mentioned here is primarily anecdotal. The purpose is to let you know what the process can *feel* like, to help you understand what your expectations should be, and to give awareness of some high-level thoughts.

Raw data, legalese, and other minutiae concerning an exit plan can be difficult to comprehend until you know the big picture. Even then, it's more important for the team you build around you to understand the raw data and what to do with it. Therefore, I'm intentionally leaving the number crunching out. That's where your exit team does one of their most important jobs—translating the little things so that you understand what it means to your sale.

The way you assemble your team is integral to the success of your exit strategy. You must have the right people in place with specific expertise, whom you trust to have your best interests in mind when performing their jobs.

The odds of you having this tool in your skill set are about to increase dramatically, as the next section will tell you—in broad terms—who you need and what they'll do.

EXIT STRATEGY TAKEAWAYS:

- There are three types of buyers to consider when selling your business: family members, employees, or third parties. Each type of buyer will bring nuances to the sale process of which you should be aware.
- Money is not the only factor when selling a business. Be sure to consider peace of mind, legacy, philanthropy, and other must-have items in your exit plan.

- Consider flexible financing when selling to an employee who might be able to assume incremental levels of ownership and responsibility.
- Third-party sales often come from within your own network, so maintain positive business relationships to maximize your odds of finding the right third-party buyer.

ROLES AND RESPONSIBILITIES: HOW TO BUILD YOUR EXIT TEAM

Do you remember what your business looked like when you first started? Did you have any employees? What about office space? What were your earnings in the first couple of years? How about the number of clients?

Businesses evolve and people change. Chances are that your business looks a lot different today than it did five, ten, twenty, or more years ago. Now a few more questions…Did you have a CPA? A lawyer? What about an investment banker? Maybe it was just you and a trusted accountant, or perhaps you had a team of professionals from the outset. If you're still working with the same people, you should do a quick fact check about whether or not those individuals can handle the sale of your business.

Some professionals and firms are better suited to smaller businesses. They prefer to deal with smaller clients for various reasons. They may not have the resources or background necessary for larger companies. Others, however, like to work with larger clients. For example, at Assante, we focus our financial advisory services on high-net-worth individuals and families. We discovered that we could create a better client experience by focusing our expertise on people who have similar issues, needs, and demands.

Now ask yourself, what about the team of people you have in place—your CPA, lawyer, etc? Has your business outgrown them? Do an honest assessment and determine if they're still the right people to help you exit the business.

What I mean by this is simple: If your business is worth $60 million and your current CPA has never handled the books for a company valued at more than $10 million, you might want to seek the advice of other CPAs. Similarly, if you have a wealth advisor or a lawyer who has never (or rarely) handled a large transaction, tap the expertise of someone who has experience with bigger deals.

Most people and firms will offer a free initial consultation to see if their services suit your needs. Reputable CPAs, wealth advisors, attorneys, and many other professionals will talk to you the first time for free. So if you feel like your business has outgrown anyone on your team, seek recommendations, gather a shortlist of people to talk to, and conduct interviews to see who can get the deal done for you with an optimal result.

YOUR EXIT TEAM NEEDS A QUARTERBACK

With an understanding that you may need a new team to help you leave your business, you need to address the team's most critical need first: the quarterback.

Every great exit team needs a quarterback—someone to take the reins, make good decisions, communicate the plan, and take appropriate actions. The role of quarterback will likely change from one team member to another, depending on which part of the sales process you're executing.

In the beginning stages, for instance, the quarterback might be your business valuator, who has to consider all the variables that go into forming a reasonable asking price for your potential buyer.

At one point in the sale, the CPA may take over as quarterback, calling the signals to ensure that proper adherence to tax mitigation is considered.

A wealth advisor, like myself, can play quarterback at any given time of the sales process because our role is not only to ensure a secure financial future, but also to seize opportunities that enhance your wealth today. We will also help you decide what to do with the money post-sale. How much will you need to account for living expenses? How much do you want to give to charity? What do you want to leave as a legacy? These questions and many others will be paramount to you enjoying your post-sale life plan. Because the answers to those questions are so impactful, choosing your wealth advisor is a big step in the right direction for the exit strategy and beyond.

Eventually a lawyer is probably going to assume the role of quarterback. They'll need to ensure all the contract language is correct and various documents are in order. Not only will they protect you against legal action, but by examining the offer and contract, they'll also ensure that your expectations for value from the deal are met.

Other people could also take over the signal calling at various points in your sales process. For instance, an insurance expert might need to be called in. Specialized attorneys like M&A lawyers and tax attorneys (whose role differs from a CPA) might also be necessary. Professionals from various industries can leverage their specific expertise to ensure the best possible outcome for you. The bottom line is that the role of quarterback could switch back and forth often. Whoever plays this role at any given time must be an excellent communicator and collaborator, capable of leading the team to victory.

COMMUNICATION IS KEY

It is difficult to determine who the correct professional is to talk to regarding the various aspects of exit strategy. Ask your current group of trusted advisors for names of people who have expertise in the various roles you'll need to fill. You can also seek referrals from other people who have already sold at least one business. If someone has had a great experience with one or more professionals, it may be wise to check into those people as possible fits for your needs.

It is important to remember that your exit team is a collaborative approach. The quarterback needs to pull everyone together so that everybody is doing their part at the right time and ensure communication is fluid throughout the team.

The CPA needs to know what the wealth advisor is doing and vice versa. In the meantime, they're both communicating with the business valuator and various attorneys.

If one of the team members isn't pulling their weight or isn't communicating well, that can be an impediment to getting the deal done on time and ensuring an optimal return. To sum it up, communication is key, and the quarterback (whoever it is at each phase) must make sure people are talking to get the job done.

KEEP A COLLABORATIVE TEAM MINDSET

Collaboration also promotes transparency and accountability. For example, if one or more of your team members tells you about an activity that's raising some red flags, you'll want to investigate. If you discover that one of your team members isn't serving your best interests, you may need to have a difficult conversation with them.

A red flag could be raised just because communication isn't flowing properly. Some team members may misinterpret certain activities if they're not letting each other know what they're doing and why they're doing it.

I can personally attest to how problematic a lack of communication can be in an exit team. Many years ago, I worked with a client who was selling their business and had a CPA who was one of their most trusted advisors. The problem was that the CPA was horrible for the rest of the team to deal with.

When I needed information to plan what the post-sale wealth management would look like, I had to wait for days—sometimes weeks—for the CPA to get back to me with what I needed. I wasn't the only one who had this problem. The client's other exit team members also had trouble getting their information from the CPA on time.

Collaboration is not only key to keeping team members happy and getting your exit strategy done in a way that doesn't cause headaches, but it's also quantifiable in terms of value. The client wanted to sell their business for $28 million but sold for less because the timeline kept getting pushed back. This had all created a great inconvenience for the buyer, so they wanted compensation for lost time and money. If your team isn't communicating, you might pay the price literally and figuratively.

YOU WANT TACTICIANS, NOT SALESPEOPLE

If you determine that lack of transparency or communication is a problem with one or more team members, you may need to begin a recruitment process for new talent. This could also be the case if your business has outgrown one of your team members. If that happens, you can start the recruitment process by asking for recommendations from others in your network. If you're bringing in somebody without a recommendation, ask to speak to their clients. Find out what their experience was when working with the recommended individual.

You might need to conduct interviews with more than a few individuals before finding the right person for the job.

Just a few years ago, I worked as the wealth advisor for another client who hired a firm to find a qualified buyer. His business was worth a lot of money. The firm, however, was incentivized *only* to get the deal done, collect their paycheck, and move on to the next client. The faster they closed, the faster they could get to the next deal. The faster they could get to the next deal, the more money they could bring in.

That client ended up selling his business for far less than he thought it was worth. He thought it was worth well over $20 million, but it sold for $12 million. Clearly he wasn't on the same page as the firm he hired.

It's unclear exactly how the situation with that particular client went off the rails, but I have some thoughts that might help you not to make the same mistake.

First of all, understand that competent and reputable firms and individuals value their long-term reputation over short-term profits. When interviewing them, try to see when someone is just telling you what you want to hear. Many people make shallow promises. "You want to sell your business for $200 million? Sure, we can do that," they might say without even bothering to look at your books to see that your business is worth only $20 million. That's a salesperson. You want tacticians and/or technicians, not salespeople.

Perhaps the client didn't spend enough time researching the firm they hired. If they spoke with other clients or vetted the firm through other trusted professionals within their own network, they likely would have spotted the potential for incentive bias.

It's also possible that the business—although highly valuable in any estimate—wasn't quite as valuable as the client thought it was. If this was the case, the firm they hired should have done a better job of managing expectations upfront. In one of their initial meetings, there should have been a discovery process to find out what the client thought their business was worth. If the firm felt uncomfortable with that number, they should have been forthright with the client and explained why they thought the company was worth slightly less.

Incentive bias happens when an individual or group becomes overly concerned with collecting on their stake in the game and sacrifices the success of the team for their own personal reward. It can exist in any role at any time during the sale process. Another typical example could be a wealth advisor who is particularly pushy about an insurance policy. In this case, they might have some form of commission at stake, or maybe they have a friend who sells the policies. Either way, it might not be serving your best interest, and you'll need to decide if you can still trust that person or if you're better off letting them go and bringing in someone else.

The right people working together to achieve the same goal without incentive bias will know when to call on a specialist to address any areas of vulnerability like insurance or specialized legal assistance. Similarly, good team members can also spot opportunities to improve your company's value or enhance your wealth after the sale. For instance, a business valuator may spot an area in your financials that can be restructured, or a wealth advisor can suggest an investment portfolio for the money you receive.

These are just a few of the many foundational items to consider when forming your exit team. The following section tells you what that exit team should look like, who should be on it, and what they'll do for your sale.

THE STRUCTURE OF YOUR EXIT TEAM

A big part of proper planning comes down to having the right people on your team. Having them in place at the time of your exit strategy is essential; having them in your network at the beginning of your business is even better. If you haven't already, you'll need to consider onboarding some or all (depending mainly on the size of your company) of the following people to form a successful exit strategy:

- Business valuator
- Wealth advisor
- CPA
- Corporate lawyer
- Tax attorney
- M&A lawyer
- Investment banker

You'll need a business valuator, CPA, corporate lawyer, and wealth advisor for almost any business sale, even the sale of small retail stores worth a few million or less. The last three from that list—tax attorney, M&A lawyer, and investment banker—are needed mostly for large organizations.

Now let's discuss the role each of these professionals will play in helping you to sell your business. Let's start from the top, as it only makes sense that you want to know what your business is worth before proceeding with anything else.

BUSINESS VALUATOR

Most business valuators will perform a broad range of services in the sale process. In some cases, they'll exclusively provide a valuation (tell you what your business is worth) and nothing more. For other sellers, business valuators act as strategic advisors before forming an exit strategy.

Selling a business is a strategic process; it's not as simple as placing a "For Sale" sign on the window and negotiating with the first buyer who walks through the door. When a business valuator is a strategic partner, they can assist in tax planning, negotiation, and due diligence.

Business valuators can also consult with the owner and management to prepare for the eventual sale. When they engage with the business early on, they can prime its marketability. They'll help people drive value well in advance of any intentions to sell.

Forming strategic partnerships should be considered with all your team members.

Even if you're not bringing in a business valuator before thinking about your exit strategy, it's still a good idea to periodically get a valuation done, as it's easy to become detached from what your business is worth.

Many people treat their business like their "baby," and who can blame them? They've likely poured their heart and soul into this entity for many years. However, a problem can arise when it comes to determining value if business owners become so enamored with their "baby" that they let their bias inflate their perceived value of it.

What happens when this person runs their business for ten or twelve years, assumes its value is around $30 million, and is informed by a professional that it's only worth around $12 million? That business owner will start their exit strategy in a negative mindset. They may begrudgingly stick to their inflated price point and do nothing but frustrate themselves and potential buyers. By getting a valuation done every few years, your expectations will always be aligned with the realities of the current market. If you have a good team of professionals working together, they will adjust to changes the business valuator sees and collaborate on how to prime the company for optimal value.

A good business valuator is a great place to start your exit strategy. After all, how can you sell your business for top dollar if you don't know what top dollar is?

Selling for top dollar is always nice, but the valuation process must be objective, as an inflated value based on the owner's wishes will only make the process more difficult, if not impossible. As with most exit strategy processes, a tactical approach is best.

The valuator will use financial statements, key metrics, valuation multiples based on earnings, and other resources unique to your business to develop a range of value. From there, you can discuss various pricing strategies with your business valuator. You might want to start low and hope to encourage bidding from multiple buyers. Or you could set your asking price on the higher end of the range, hoping to streamline the process by only getting attention from the most serious buyers.

A good business valuator is essential to selling your business. However, a good wealth advisor is an equally valuable team member. This person will assist in managing and protecting your wealth before and after the sale. For many business owners, the wealth advisor becomes their most trusted team member.

THE WEALTH ADVISOR

The wealth advisor is an umbrella term that includes stockbrokers and investment managers. Unlike a business valuator, stockbrokers and investment managers don't usually get involved with presale exit planning. They'll recommend things to do with your money as a *reactive* strategy: their involvement is solely after the funds clear. These people are product-driven and will have recommendations for ways to distribute your wealth post-sale, but don't usually get involved with an exit strategy.

The investment aspect of your post-sale funds is important, but so is tax mitigation, protecting your wealth, and distributing it properly into charitable donations and philanthropic vehicles. Therefore, many clients need a wealth advisor with a more comprehensive service offering and an iterative process that involves a structured timeline that allows you to collaborate with a team of professionals on an advanced plan customized to your unique situation.

Wealth Management Consultative Process

- TWO WEEKS -

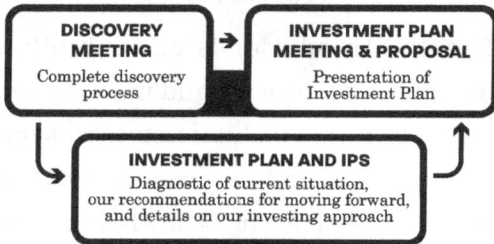

DISCOVERY MEETING

Complete discovery process

→

INVESTMENT PLAN MEETING & PROPOSAL

Presentation of Investment Plan

INVESTMENT PLAN AND IPS

Diagnostic of current situation, our recommendations for moving forward, and details on our investing approach

- ONE WEEK -

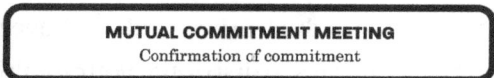

MUTUAL COMMITMENT MEETING

Confirmation of commitment

- POST 45-90 DAYS -

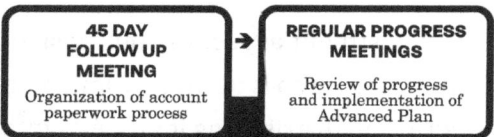

45 DAY FOLLOW UP MEETING

Organization of account paperwork process

→

REGULAR PROGRESS MEETINGS

Review of progress and implementation of Advanced Plan

- ADVANCED PLAN -

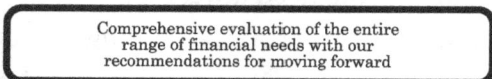

Comprehensive evaluation of the entire range of financial needs with our recommendations for moving forward

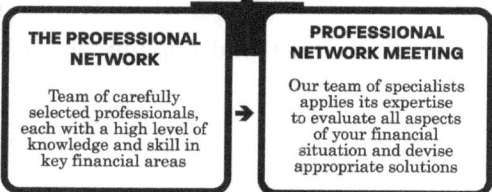

THE PROFESSIONAL NETWORK

Team of carefully selected professionals, each with a high level of knowledge and skill in key financial areas

→

PROFESSIONAL NETWORK MEETING

Our team of specialists applies its expertise to evaluate all aspects of your financial situation and devise appropriate solutions

At Assante, a few advisors—myself included—like to use a unique approach with our clients. We will work on a consultative basis with you as part of a proactive strategy. Being proactive allows us to get involved in the exit planning process. We'll work collaboratively with the rest of your team—the CPA, the tax lawyer, and even the business valuator—to form a more advanced planning spectrum. Most advisors don't include this type of service in their offering, but it will likely behoove you to find one who does.

Wealth management solutions could include what to do with a Registered Retirement Savings Plan (RRSP) or Individual Pension Plan (IPP), which is better. There could also be a Retirement Compensation Arrangement (RCA) or a dividend income split with a spouse once the business owner reaches age sixty-five. Understanding these options in-depth can also help you to mitigate taxes when exiting your business. A more detailed discussion of these items is provided later in a section called "Tax Planning." The critical thing to remember about these solutions is to consult with a trusted professional who can help you understand the best option(s) for your unique situation.

Integrated wealth management planning involves tax, legal, estate, investment, and financial planning, all of which are essential throughout the life cycle of the business.

There are a lot of wealth transfer issues to consider, such as when to transfer the wealth, an update of taxation at death, structuring and restructuring wills and trusts, equalization between family members, and more. Everyone will have a couple of wealth transfer issues. It's simply a matter of which ones apply to you.

Wealth protection is a way of mitigating risk so something unforeseen doesn't derail your sale process. A wealth advisor uses proven strategies to protect your wealth and ensure your assets are not unjustly taken through litigation. In other words, if a divorce occurs in the middle of a sale or somebody files a case against you for property/casualty, you'll be covered. To do this, sometimes a wealth advisor will bring in an insurance specialist.

If your wealth advisor is also tapping their network for potential buyers, you'll want to find out to whom they'll be pitching your business. Probe your wealth advisor on their capabilities. Whether you're looking for someone to simply manage your wealth after the sale or a strategic partner to help during the sale, find out what the person you're talking with can do.

Personally, I like to say that I operate as my clients' personal Chief Financial Officer (CFO). Together, we will discover where the money should go and how it fits in relation to your goals and objectives for personal spending, heirs, your estate, and philanthropic wishes. Consider the following Wealth Management Formula as a foundational understanding of all the aspects of your personal wealth that should be considered by your wealth advisor.

The Wealth Management Formula

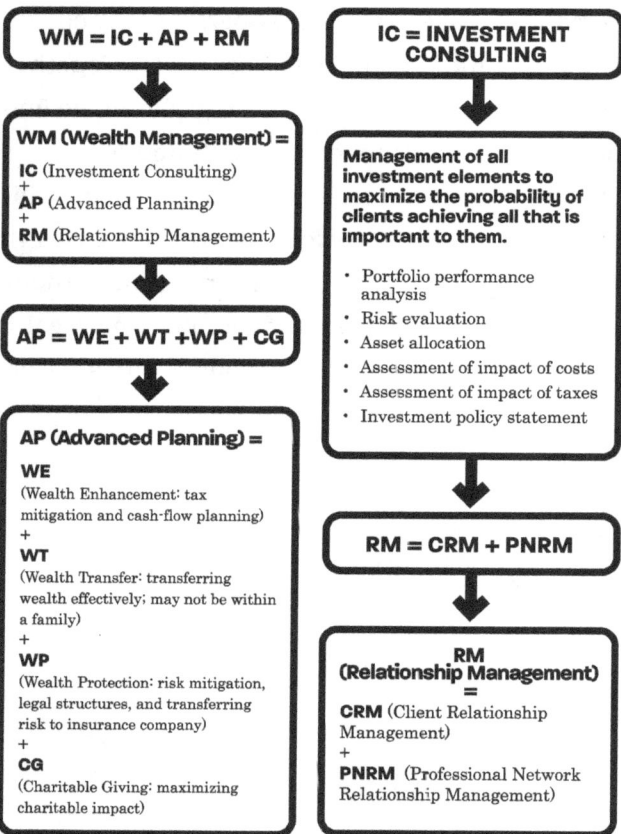

WM = IC + AP + RM

WM (Wealth Management) =
IC (Investment Consulting)
+
AP (Advanced Planning)
+
RM (Relationship Management)

AP = WE + WT + WP + CG

AP (Advanced Planning) =

WE
(Wealth Enhancement: tax mitigation and cash-flow planning)
+
WT
(Wealth Transfer: transferring wealth effectively; may not be within a family)
+
WP
(Wealth Protection: risk mitigation, legal structures, and transferring risk to insurance company)
+
CG
(Charitable Giving: maximizing charitable impact)

IC = INVESTMENT CONSULTING

Management of all investment elements to maximize the probability of clients achieving all that is important to them.

- Portfolio performance analysis
- Risk evaluation
- Asset allocation
- Assessment of impact of costs
- Assessment of impact of taxes
- Investment policy statement

RM = CRM + PNRM

RM (Relationship Management) =
CRM (Client Relationship Management)
+
PNRM (Professional Network Relationship Management)

After discovering the capabilities of your wealth advisor, you should also test for incentive bias, as it can exist with wealth advisors as well as any other team member. One way you can do this is to understand how the compensation for your wealth advisor works. Ask them if they get paid based on the sale's success (which is often the case), if it's a flat rate, or if it follows some other structure.

THE CPA

Another key member of just about every exit team is the CPA. Tax mitigation is a more significant concern than most business owners realize. After all, you are transferring an asset worth millions of dollars. This is how a common error in exit planning occurs, as many business owners focus on maximizing the purchase price and don't pay enough attention to tax advice.

The CPA will usually start their process by sending a memo to your lawyer stating their intentions to set up your corporate structure in a way that will be most beneficial for tax purposes during the sale of your business. If you already have a CPA on staff, make sure they're doing this before going any

further in the sale process. If the proper tax structure isn't set up in time, this could cost you a lot of
money in the long run.

A good CPA should caution you against attempting
overly aggressive tax behavior. Although differences
exist between the Canada Revenue Agency (CRA) in
Canada and the Internal Revenue Service (IRS) in the
US, both agencies have experts constantly looking
for red flags indicating the possible exploitation of
tax laws. Mostly, they're not looking to find out that
Grandma didn't declare $1,000 earnings in childcare.
Rather, they're interested in searching every detail of
a business transaction that involves millions of dollars. Selling your business falls under this category,
so be prepared for appropriate scrutiny.

When selling your business, you can opt to maximize tax savings upfront, and risk spending tens of
thousands of dollars on a CPA or a tax lawyer later
to defend that decision in an audit. When you see as
many cases of this as I do—or better yet, as a good
CPA does—you realize how an overly aggressive tax
strategy is usually a poor business decision.

A good CPA will present you with all the options

pertaining to tax laws. They'll examine your risk profile and explain the advantages and disadvantages of your choices. Most importantly, a CPA will tell you how to sell your business in a way that is both tax-effective and does not raise any red flags.

What happens if you have a cross-border operation in Canada and the US?

In the US, a lot of people like to set up limited liability companies (LLC). In Canada, you are currently taxed at approximately 70 percent on those, so if you have a CPA in the US and another one in Canada, they need to communicate on how to set that up for sale. If they don't collaborate, you could end up paying significantly more taxes than you need to.

One of the CPAs I spoke with told me a story about a client who has a business in Canada and mining space in the US. The client wasn't sure if they were properly advised when they set up the LLC in the US based on their Canadian citizenship.

The client didn't expect the business to do as well as it did. It became worth around $500 million in the first year, so it was successful beyond their wildest dreams. Unfortunately, their tax liability in Canada is 70 percent of that figure due to the LLC they set up in the US.

Was this the CPA's fault? Was it wrongdoing by an attorney?

After going through the emails and notes from the various meetings, everyone agreed that the client was correctly advised. The tax lawyer had laid out all the options for the client, told them about the advantages and disadvantages, and the client chose the most straightforward option because they were too busy to give it the necessary consideration.

This sort of thing happens all the time. People get focused on one aspect of their business and end up paying in the long run. It's hard to place blame in a situation like that, because the client is trying to do everything they can to get the business up and running; they're probably working sixteen-hour days and don't always have the time to give certain aspects of their business the attention they need. Meanwhile, the professionals are normally performing due diligence in trying to translate the information for them. Unfortunately, the best decision doesn't always jump out to people right away.

CORPORATE LAWYER

The simple act of opening a company can require several legal documents depending on the type of business and where it's operating, among other factors. You might have a family lawyer you use for business and/or personal reasons. If you have a deep trust in that person—a confidence in their knowledge of tax laws and estate planning—they may be enough to handle the legal side of your exit plan as well. This isn't always the case, however.

If you began working with this person when your business was worth $3 million, and today it's worth $30 million, your business might have outgrown their expertise. If this is the case, start interviewing bigger firms with people who have handled the legal side of an exit plan for more valuable businesses.

If your business is a corporation, remember that a corporate lawyer will serve the best interest of the corporation, not necessarily the business owner.

If you're not familiar with what a corporate lawyer does, the following definition works well: "business or corporate lawyers are tasked with ensuring a company's transactions comply with corporate laws and regulations. They may work at a law firm or as part of a company's legal team. Duties include preparing documents, assessing partnerships, and negotiating deals."[1]

A corporate lawyer will usually begin their part of the exit strategy by taking a financial snapshot of the business. The big picture perspective helps them to grasp the value of the company. After understanding the value, they'll ask you questions about what you think the business is worth and what you want your retirement to look like before they dig deeper into how the company is structured.

You want a corporate lawyer who is good at listening to their clients' needs. They should have a deep understanding of your specific situation. If they're not asking questions to determine what you want to get out of the sale, there's likely an incentive bias to "just get the deal done."

---

1   Learn more about the job requirements and skills of a corporate lawyer at https://www.betterteam.com/corporate-lawyer-job-description.

So if your team is asking questions, it's a good thing. It shows their dedication. With that in mind, you want to be as transparent as possible with every team member, especially your business attorney, who will be there to defend you if any litigation takes place. Teamwork is much more impactful when everybody knows what the ultimate goal is.

Lawyers of various areas of expertise could be present in any particular business sale. Of particular interest is the tax lawyer. This person shouldn't be confused with the CPA, as their specific roles differ.

TAX LAWYER

A tax lawyer looks at things through a slightly different lens than a CPA. In my experience, tax lawyers are more focused on mitigating overall risk to the client. They'll look through shareholder agreements and make sure that warranties and representations are properly structured. Tax lawyers can help a startup create and review the business structure so that personal assets are properly protected.

Subtle but distinct and important differences exist between a corporate lawyer and a tax lawyer. Consider bringing in a tax lawyer on any deal worth over $20 million. This is not a rule set in stone. Rather it is a ballpark estimate. Some deals will be worth much more but may not require a tax lawyer; others may be worth slightly less but still worth the cost. Explore your options, consult with other trusted team members, and decide whether a tax lawyer is needed for your deal or not.

Depending on the complexity of the business and the deal at hand, tax lawyers are better equipped to maximize the lifetime capital gains exemption (LCGE). They can also assist you in understanding and minimizing risks throughout your exit strategy, as well as help you to sort through your minute book and get it optimally prepared for review by potential buyers.

To prevent a deal from going sideways in a large organization, the tax lawyer can be well worth the fees. If the deal is big enough, you may also need an M&A lawyer who specializes in large transactions.

MERGERS AND ACQUISITIONS (M&A) LAWYER

Typically, you won't need an M&A lawyer unless

your business is worth $30 million or more. These legal experts provide tremendous value at an appropriately high fee. If your business is worth that kind of dollar figure and you bring in an M&A lawyer, a big part of the value they provide is in the network they bring with them.

M&A lawyers will often spearhead the entire process if engaged early. In other words, they might take on the role of quarterback and keep it, while only handing the ball off to a team member when necessary. They likely have someone who can handle most or all aspects of your sale process without needing to involve anyone else. For instance, they'll be able to bring in a tax attorney, an insurance specialist, an investment banker, etc. An M&A lawyer is a one-stop shop, but your business must be worth an appropriate value.

If your books are a mess or nonexistent, the M&A lawyer will provide great assistance in getting them in order. This full-service provider will help you understand what each stage of the sale process looks like and what you should think about when it happens. They'll talk to you about the purchase price, representations, and how you will cash out.

Because the role of an M&A lawyer is so compre-hensive, it helps if you bring them in right away. If you decide to sell your business and you know it's worth at least $30 million, try calling an M&A lawyer. If you think they're a good fit for your needs, get them started as soon as possible because they'll need time to perform their value-added services.

INVESTMENT BANKER

An investment banker is another role you may not need to fill unless you are selling a large business.

Investment bankers usually begin their process by doing a deep discovery with the founder to uncover their goals and objectives. This is how they'll decide on timelines, agree on what the business is worth, and discuss who the potential buyers are and what current bids might be on the table. The deep discovery is a pivotal step to avoiding any miscom-munication about expectations.

A highly esteemed investment banker I have worked with has told me that their objective in helping a client sell a business is to provide trust-worthy advice on strategy, tactics, and valuation work, among other aspects of the sale. In this way, they may provide a one-stop-shop experience.

That same individual has said that selling a business is usually more work than the business owner realizes. Doing it while running the business can feel overwhelming. Part of their service offering is to remove this overwhelm from your plate. They keep their eye on financials to ensure your company delivers on its forecast. This will keep potential buyers interested and stop them from using a downward trend against you in negotiations. A recent historical track record of growth is essential to maximizing the value of your sale.

EXIT STRATEGY TAKEAWAYS

- Everything in an exit plan is situational. There is no one-size-fits-all plan.
- Trust, collaboration, and proactivity are key to forming an effective exit team.
- You want tacticians on your team, not salespeople.
- Consider an M&A lawyer and investment banker only when selling a large business.

- Put a collaborative team in place that combines expertise related to taxes, legal issues, and business advice. You want many brains operating as one.

START PLANNING YOUR EXIT TODAY

Every business owner thinks about when they should start their exit plan at some point. Some imagine walking away far off in the future because they want to run their business until they reach retirement age. Others (serial entrepreneurs) want to sell quickly so they can move on to their next venture.

Whatever your situation as a business owner is, there is one cardinal rule to remember about exit planning: the sooner, the better.

An esteemed CPA colleague said that the biggest problem he encounters is when a business owner doesn't plan soon enough. More than one person familiar with what it takes to sell a business has told me, "The day you get into business is the day you should start planning your exit."

Many business owners casually dismiss the idea that selling their business ideally takes around five years. They figure they'll find a buyer, and six months later, they'll hand over the keys and walk off into the sunset. It's not that easy. But it doesn't need to be stressful or overly complex. I collected the following list of to-do items from several exit strategy experts:

- First, you need to find out if your business is even sellable. If so, is now the right time according to market conditions? Do you envision the timing being better in a few years or more? Does that even matter to you? The market may not be as important as the timing of your personal situation.
- Get educated about selling your business. You don't need to know all the details about tax laws and contract terms, but you need to be able to speak the same language as the people you hire to do those things.
- Forget what you *think* your business is worth. Find out what it is actually worth from a professional who has a proven process for evaluating

companies. Ask them how they arrived at that figure and ask yourself if that figure satisfies your needs and expectations.

- Be aware of when to focus on price and when to focus on the tax side of the sale. Tax implications are usually more crucial for smaller businesses—valuations of $5-$10 million. Most companies worth more than that should focus on price. However, every situation is unique, and the business owner should rely on their team to help them understand the correct area of focus.

- Understand how price and structure work in today's business environment. Many business owners believe they have a great deal. But, after viewing the structure, they realize it's worth far less than they initially thought due to the after-tax basis.

- Take a look at your books. Are they up-to-date? Buyers want transparency and a proven track record of growth. If they can't look at your books and make sense of how you're making money, there's a good chance they'll get scared off. Buyers don't like risk.

- If you're trying to maximize value, it's important not to rush the sale. Bad health, a desire to sell by the end of the year, and a million other reasons exist to set an ambitious deadline for the sale of your business. You can make that thing happen, but you won't get top dollar. If you rush the sale, be prepared to obtain a lower purchase price. Savvy buyers will sniff out motivation to get out fast and use it as a negotiation tactic.

What that list leaves out is *how* you'll find a buyer. Remember, this could be a family member, an employee, or a third party. If a third party is your choice, you'll need to think about how you'll market your business.

MARKETING MATERIAL: LET THE WORLD KNOW YOUR BUSINESS IS FOR SALE

How do you plan to get the word out that your business is for sale? Not all business owners know where or how to find potential buyers. You can hire a firm (as mentioned previously) to search their network and find a good fit for you. You can also search your own network. Whether searching your network or someone else's, consider putting together a teaser document to let the world know you're open for bids.

Different professionals may be able to put together

this marketing material, but the most common source to get it done is a business valuator.

Many potential buyers may not know a lot about your operations, especially if you're in a niche industry. The purpose of the teaser document (also referred to as a business summary document) is to educate buyers about your business.

The teaser document is just what it sounds like. It contains enough information to provide a teaser of interest. It is only one or two pages in length and provides the company's unique selling points while clearly stating the value of the business.

Business valuators can also draw up a document with a little more detail called a confidential information memorandum (CIM). It provides a potential buyer with an in-depth look at the company, including (but not limited to):

- Overview and key investment highlights
- A description of products and services
- A snapshot of the overall market
- Sales and marketing data
- A look at the management team

- Past financial results and future projections
- Risk factors

Not every teaser document or CIM will include the same information. Selling a business is always situational. Every seller is different and so is every buyer. The terms and conditions change based on timing, industry, and other factors.

Work with your team on how to best position your business for sale through marketing material and the other resources at your disposal. Once again, communication is vital. Make sure everyone is on the same page. The first words on that page should convey, "The business has a good existing structure."

A SOLID STRUCTURE WILL ACCELERATE THE SALE

"If a business is not structured properly for sale," a CPA friend has mentioned, "restructuring could be needed, which takes considerable time and resources. For example, if you are restructuring to multiply the capital gains exemption using your spouse and children, you need time for growth to occur in the business after restructuring."

Another dilemma many business owners face is whether or not they should pay early to set up the structure properly and maintain it. This will have the business ready for sale at any time (given that all other variables are in place).

We don't like to think about things like mortality, but have you thought about how the transition of your business would take shape if something were to happen to you? Some business owners understandably seize the short-term advantage of not paying for a solid structure up front. However, unforeseen circumstances often pop up that can make it costlier (in terms of a delayed sale, undesirable litigation, or a transition you never wanted) in the long term. If cash flow allows, the safe bet is to pay the fees upfront to put a good structure in place. Then, review that structure periodically to ensure it still accurately reflects the situation since the last review. These proactive steps will save you a lot of money in the long term.

Beware of shortsightedness. Business owners who can streamline their day-to-day operations, while keeping their vision for the future crystal clear are set up for success today, tomorrow, and beyond. One of the best ways to think long-term is to keep clean books.

CLEAN BOOKS ADD CURB APPEAL

Most business owners have little idea of what it means to clean up the accounting side. They don't understand how important it is to remove inactive or redundant assets. In case you're unfamiliar, a redundant asset is an asset that generates income but is not linked to the fundamental operations of the company.[2] The same holds true for bookkeeping. Business owners also need to be aware of normalizing personal expenses and understand the tax implications of selling.

When selling your business, your books are akin to the curb appeal of selling a house. If a prospective home buyer shows up for a showing and finds structural damage in the basement, they're almost certainly not going to buy the house. At the least, they will ask for a substantial discount to pay for the repairs, and the closing will probably get delayed until the buyer is satisfied with the reconciliation.

The same result occurs if a potential buyer looks at your books and sees red flags about performance, redundant assets, or how the business operates.

---

2   Paul Tracy, "Redundant Asset," *InvestingAnswers*, October 1, 2019, https://investinganswers.com/dictionary/r/redundant-asset.

Subsequently, they may ask for some restructuring of the business and a deeper probe into how it works—all of which takes additional time.

I've personally seen how troublesome messy financial statements can be for the seller. One of my clients, Daniel, put a solid team together and got a great price for a business he owned for thirty years. He ended up selling for over $18 million.

Daniel had a business partner. While they owned the business, they drew annual salaries of close to $400,000, but there was also another $180,000 in discretionary expenses paid by the company. This isn't unethical or even uncommon. Travel, smartphones, internet access, real estate, cash, and investments are common redundant assets between business and personal expenses.

The problem with redundant assets is that they all need to be stripped out before a sale. They also must be separated after the sale for your life plan going forward. Daniel and I had to meet numerous times to go over every line item of his books. After the deal, we had to determine what he needed to spend from his portfolio.

There can be no blending of personal or discretionary spending with business expenses if you want to get the highest possible price. We call this "noise" on the income statement. The more noise on the financials, the less clear it is for the buyer to see profitability or growth.

Noise can also become a massive nuisance to the buyer in the post-sale phase. They have to separate the personal expenses of the previous owner from the business expenses. Otherwise, they're dealing with what we call redundant assets. This sort of thing happens a lot, and the savvy buyer will not want to deal with it.

What usually happens is the buyer will spot the redundant assets during the negotiation process and use it for leverage. They'll ask for a discount as restitution for cleaning up the seller's books and normalizing the business earnings. Unclean books present an element of risk. If the books aren't updated consistently, the true value of the business may not be what it initially appears to be.

If you haven't maintained clean books or completely ignored them, don't waste time lamenting your oversight any further. You can't change what has already happened. Business owners are busy people; I'm sure you're no exception. There are many issues to consider when starting a business, many more to grow it, and perhaps even more to sell it.

Even if you're not considering the sale of your business for many years, get the books straightened out now. That way, you won't have a monumental task before you can put together a reasonable exit strategy. One of the books every business owner should have at their disposal during their ownership of the business and when getting it ready for sale is the minute book.

THE MINUTE BOOK

One of the most (if not the most) important pieces of documentation to keep clean is your minute book. If you're unsure of what I mean by a minute book, it is something almost every buyer will want to see as soon as they express interest in your business.

A minute book is essentially a corporate binder containing the company's resolutions, shareholder ledger, articles of incorporation, list of directors, by-laws, and all internal corporate documents of the company.[3]

Two of the critical pieces of information a seller is looking to get from a minute book are how the corporation is set up and who the shareholders are.

Even if you're not considering the sale of your business for many years, you should make it a habit to update your minute book every year. If you currently have no minute book or it hasn't been updated in a long time, it probably isn't worth anything to the buyer. Even if you're not considering the sale of your business for many years, a lender will often want to see portions of the minute book. So if you plan on borrowing money, get your minute book in order regardless of whether you're selling your business today or in thirty years.

If it seems too time-consuming to annually update your minute book while running your business, hire someone to do it for you. This person may only take small pieces of your time to discuss the information they need to establish or straighten out the document. Still, outsourcing

---

3 "Minute Book: What Is a Corporate Book and Why It's Important," *incorporated.zone (blog)*, June 16, 2020, https://incorporated.zone/minute-book-what-is-a-corporate-book-and-why-its-important/.

this task will save you time, and even though you will pay fees upfront, a substantial return on investment will come back to you when you sell the business.

Companies with updated and clean books sell faster because they have the equivalent of curb appeal, which translates to higher value. The bonus factor is the time-liness with which the deal can get done.

HAVE MANAGEMENT IN PLACE FOR A SMOOTH TRANSITION

Another way to de-risk the business for buyers is to ensure a strong management team is in place and that they will remain there after the sale. A buyer wants to be able to lean on people, post-sale, who know the business inside and out.

Most buyers will not have intimate knowledge of how your business runs, especially since every business has some level of nuance. They may not have much knowledge of the industry.

There are always different relationships, systems, and processes that exist from one business to the next. A buyer will want to be sure that someone who knows those things will stick around to help them as they make the transition.

For some business owners, having capable management on hand isn't a problem; they've had brilliant people learning the business with them for years. Some people like to take on an apprentice and teach them everything they know. There's an element of mentorship that is fulfilling to them.

If you're fortunate enough to be surrounded by talented, hard-working people, it's important not to lose them during the sale process. Even the best management teams can become distracted during a transition of ownership. Some may fear how their roles may change, while others may worry if they will have a job at all. Many executives will wonder how their new relationships with the new owners will work. These are all entirely normal human emotions, and as their leader, you must help assure them (if possible) of their job security after the sale.

Distracted management can be quite detrimental to the value of your sale, as buyers will be looking to ensure your company delivers on its forecast. If they see your books have estimated a reasonable profit for the quarter leading up to the sale and you don't meet that goal, it may affect your sale price by more than you think.

Management personnel who get distracted is one problem to consider, but it's an even bigger problem if you don't have anybody who knows how to handle the business without you. Some business owners struggle with letting someone get too close to their business, preferring to operate as more of a one-person show.

If a buyer sees that you wear too many hats in your company, it may work against you. They might fear being left on an island when they take ownership. Buyers want skilled, trained, and dedicated people already on the staff, especially on the management side, when they take over the business. The more great people the buyer sees working for you, the more leverage you'll have in the purchase price.

If you don't already have people in place who can keep operations running smoothly while the transition of ownership takes place, find them as soon as possible. This should be at or near the top of your to-do list for your exit strategy (right after having clean books).

Absorb whatever initial cost it takes to recruit, hire, and train expertise on the management side of your business. Work closely with your new hires until they can maintain operations without you. With a target date of three to five years out to fully execute your exit strategy, you should still have plenty of time to find the right people and bring them up to speed.

With the right people in place, you must discuss a strategy around tax planning, as it is crucial to the success of every business sale.

TAX PLANNING

Tax planning comes up as a consideration from every professional I've spoken with about forming a solid exit strategy. A friend and colleague, Brandon Lewis, who is a business valuator and a CPA, told me that proper tax planning is worth every penny. With that in mind, the sale of an incorporated business can be transacted in three forms:

1. Assets
2. Shares
3. Hybrid of shares and assets

The decision to transact an asset sale versus shares requires consideration of many tax and nontax factors, as both play a significant role in the decision.

A SHARE SALE VERSUS AN ASSET SALE

Sellers and buyers often reside on opposite ends of the spectrum when negotiating whether a corporation will be sold via shares or assets. Sellers prefer a share-based agreement. On the other end of the table, however, buyers usually benefit from an asset-based sale. An asset purchase will usually result in an increase to the cost base of the assets of the business, which provides a greater cost base upon which depreciation may be claimed for tax purposes.

An asset purchase can be a more complex transaction to implement because each asset must be transferred and registered in the name of the buyer. From a risk perspective, buying the assets of an existing corporation and transferring them to a new corporation means the buyer will only inherit liabilities they specifically assume with the operating assets. This could become a concern if the nature of the business lent itself to a recognition of significant potential unrecorded liabilities (e.g., environmental damage).

Whether transacting a sale of shares or assets, there is a multitude of opportunities for the seller to minimize tax. Let's begin by discussing a few tax mitigation strategies for a share-based sale.

THE LIFETIME CAPITAL GAINS EXEMPTION (LCGE)

Most business owners prefer to sell shares because it's simpler, the corporate liabilities stay with the corporation post-sale, and the lifetime capital gains exemption (LCGE) may be available, which could significantly reduce the tax burden on the seller.

Business owners can shelter a significant portion of the profit from the sale of qualified small business shares by claiming the LCGE. There are rules, however, around what types of businesses qualify for such tax planning. Ensuring that your business qualifies cannot be done overnight.

A fair amount of legalese is necessary to accurately describe the exact qualifications for claiming an

LCGE. If any of this feels outside of your comfort zone, it is best to write down questions and seek the advice of a trusted team member, like a CPA or tax attorney.

For starters, you must be a resident of Canada throughout the year to claim the LCGE. (For US business owners, ask your CPA or tax attorney about which rules may apply.) A lifetime capital gain exemption for an individual is currently set at $913,630 for 2022 and is annually indexed for inflation. An individual shareholder could shelter over $200,000 of taxes, depending on the province or territory in which the individual is a resident. The amount you can claim is reduced in accordance with LCGE claims from previous taxation years. Further, the LCGE could also be reduced by any net capital losses claimed—allowable business investment losses (ABIL)—and any cumulative net investment loss at the end of the year.

In growing or mature businesses, taxes become an increasingly prominent concern. Most business owners have a significant percentage of wealth tied up in investments, particularly in real estate that may be subject to creditors, which could disqualify the use of the LCGE. There are ways to plan around this. For instance, you could have a separate holding company for your real estate and investments, which will purify your operating company (OpCo). This relates to the movement of redundant assets discussed earlier from OpCo to a holding company (HoldCo) to a new holding company (NewCo).

The best tax strategies often depend on what you are selling. Will you be selling shares of OpCo, HoldCo, or both? If HoldCo is involved, you will likely need to restructure and transfer investment accounts not related to a NewCo.

To qualify for the LCGE, you must also dispose of a share of a qualified small business corporation (QSBC). This is defined as a share of the capital stock of a corporation that meets the following criteria:

1. **The Determination Time Asset Test**—At any time (the determination time), you own the share as part of a small business corporation (SBC). To qualify as an SBC, it is required that the corporation be considered a Canadian-controlled private corporation (CCPC); all or a substantial portion (90 percent) of the fair

market value of the assets are used in an active business conducted primarily in Canada by the corporation or a related corporation; or certain shares and indebtedness of a connected SBC; or any combination of such assets.

2. **The Twenty-Four-Month Ownership Test—** The share was not owned by anyone unrelated to the individual during the twenty-four months prior to the determination time.

3. **The Twenty-Four-Month Asset Test—**When the situation involves only one corporation (i.e., not a holding company that owns an operating company), in the twenty-four months preceding the determination time, the fair market value of the assets of which must have been attributable to assets used principally in an active business carried on primarily in Canada by the corporation or a related corporation, or certain shares or indebtedness of a connected corporation, or any combination of such assets. When the share being considered is that of a holding corporation, additional considerations apply, and the twenty-four-month asset test may be more stringent.

A determination of eligible or non-eligible assets for

purposes of the tests described previously must be made with consideration of all facts related to the specific business. For example, a seasonal business may require a greater proportion of cash or investment assets.

If a corporation does not meet the twenty-four-month test, various strategies exist to "purify" the corporation. Purification amounts to removing excess non-eligible assets. However, it can take up to two years or more for the shares to satisfy the QSBC definition after purification. Therefore, a sense of urgency exists to review the status of your corporation's shares to transact an efficient exit strategy. It would also be crucial to examine this issue as part of the planning in an estate freeze. Once again, it is highly recommended to consult with a trusted member of your team for the best advice for your specific situation regarding any of this information.

Usage of Multiple Exemptions

An additional tax planning strategy exists for sellers of shares to name children and other family members as shareholders of the corporation. This typically happens through the use of a family trust as part of a corporate reorganization or estate freeze.

If the value of the corporation's shares increases after an estate freeze and they are sold at a later date, the family members would incur a capital gain proportionate to the value of the shares they hold—directly or indirectly through a family trust—and may potentially shelter any tax otherwise payable on the capital gain by using their own LCGE. A fair warning exists with this strategy in that it requires planning far in advance of a share sale.

Payments from Available Tax Pools

Another tax planning strategy is to remove value from the corporation in a more tax-conscious manner prior to the sale. There are two ways of pursuing this technique:

1. **Shareholder Loans**—Your corporation can repay amounts owed to shareholders without tax. If possible, these amounts should be repaid prior to a sale. While these repayments have zero effect on the potential purchase price (i.e., they result in an equal decrease in the assets

and liabilities of the corporation), they provide the shareholders with additional cash on a tax-free basis.

2. **Capital Dividend Account**—You can distribute the balance of the corporation's capital dividend account (CDA) to your shareholders on a tax-free basis. The CDA usually arises from three possible sources: The tax-free portion (50 percent) of any net capital gains realized by the corporation, life insurance proceeds received by the corporation, and/or capital dividends received by the corporation.

Once again, consult with a trusted team member when evaluating all of the tax planning strategies mentioned here, as different thoughts often arise given the unique circumstances that surround any individual business. Now let's discuss the various strategies for tax mitigation around an asset-based sale.

Allocation of Purchase Price

When considering an asset-based sale, the allocation of the purchase price amongst the assets being sold becomes a key issue. For the buyer, it is important to maximize the tax cost of the assets being purchased. This will equip them with the most beneficial write-off of the tax cost over time via tax depreciation. The buyer may therefore place greater emphasis on obtaining tax cost base for depreciable property (e.g., buildings and equipment) rather than non-depreciable items (e.g., land).

For sellers, the most beneficial tax position may differ significantly depending on the nature of the assets being sold. A seller will ultimately want to allocate the purchase price toward assets that trigger capital gains alone (e.g., land and goodwill) versus those that recapture depreciation (e.g., most depreciable property).

Any allocation, however, cannot be driven solely by tax considerations of the buyer or seller. The fair market value of the property and regulations applicable to these issues under the Canadian Income Tax Act must be factored into any allocation of assets. (In the US, check for similar federal regulations.).

Individual Pension Plans (IPP)

IPPs became popular when the federal government

introduced major pension reform legislation in 1990. They differ from the more common registered pension plan (RPP) in that an IPP doesn't pertain to a group of employees. They solely apply to an individual or an individual and their family members.

The major advantage of an IPP is the additional tax-sheltered savings that can be created in comparison to a registered retirement savings plan (RRSP). The additional contribution allowance is available because an IPP is usually established as a defined benefit plan, as opposed to a defined contribution plan (also known as a money purchase plan). As with most business-related considerations, various advantages and disadvantages exist:

Advantages:

- Contributions in excess of normal RRSP limits
- Potential ability to make lump sum payment past service contributions
- Creditor protection
- Terminal funding payments
- Bridge funding payments
- Interest deductibility of payments to IPP
- Executive owns the surplus

- Possible intergenerational transfer of pension assets
- Additional contributions allowed if plan deficit occurs
- Locked-in feature prevents access to funds until retirement

Disadvantages:

- Costs related to set-up, annual filing, and valuation fees
- Complexity
- Liquidity restriction of funds
- Reduced RRSP allowance
- No spousal contributions
- Funding requirements for an employer
- Potential for required minimum payments at age seventy-one

Retirement Compensation Agreements (RCA)

RCAs are a useful way to provide for the retirement of a key employee, including the owner-manager of a business. These agreements can provide tax benefits when the employee expects to be taxed at a lower marginal rate after retirement.

An RCA can be established when the employer (or other eligible contributor) contributes an amount to the custodian under the terms of the plan or arrangement. The custodian must obtain two account numbers: one is an RCA account number, the other is from the CRA for the plan.

RCA agreements tend to be highly specialized and complex. They require a deep dive into the advantages and disadvantages with a trusted member of your team.

ESTATE PLANNING

A consistent theme should be starting to develop as you continue reading—exit strategy requires plenty of planning. I say a three-year timeline is a rush job (although possible), and five years is realistic because there are so many considerations. You need to think about marketing, hiring a team, getting an accurate valuation, taxes, legal issues, bookkeeping, and more.

Another aspect of exit strategy that can get overlooked (especially if you don't have a good wealth advisor working for you) is estate planning. Actually, this is an aspect of making money in your business that gets overlooked. If your business is worth anything, you need to think about what happens to its value in undesirable situations.

If you don't already have an estate lawyer/attorney who has written up your will, get one. You want to protect the value of your business. Part of your exit strategy, of course, needs to include where the funds go in the event of your untimely passing. To put it bluntly, you want to make sure the right people inherit your assets, not the government or someone else you hadn't intended.

As you form your exit strategy, you'll need to consider if there are any threats around individual financial problems. Suppose a family member is inheriting the business. Are they staring down bankruptcy or something else, like a divorce, that could harm the company or the welfare of other family members who have a vested interest in the company?

Consider the business owner with three kids—each with one-third ownership of a trust set up by the owner. First, that business owner did the smart thing by having a trust set up for his children. Many people get so wrapped up in daily life that they procrastinate on this sort of thing. Unfortunately, setting up a trust may not be enough.

When people get married, we never like to think about a day when things aren't as blissful as the wedding day. But life happens. People change and relationships evolve or devolve. Losing assets to a divorce, for example, falls outside of a trust. A trust helps protect the assets and keep the wealth in the bloodline, as the trust is a separate tax-paying entity and does not form part of your matrimonial assets on the division of assets at marital dissolution.

Without a marriage contract stating exactly what happens to those shares in the event of a divorce, half of all assets brought into the marriage are claimed as marital property. At least that's the case in Canada. There may be a slight difference in the US. If you're a business owner in the States, you should ask your attorney how this and other potentially troublesome situations might affect your assets from a business sale or operation of the business.

Estate planning in many cases might involve an awkward conversation. Most business owners don't love telling their son or daughter that they need to have their fiancé sign a marriage contract that protects the inherited assets from being claimed by a scorned ex-spouse.

Most people—including many industry professionals—aren't aware of how that works. It's not something you need to consume yourself with, but it is something to think about. Get opinions from your team, colleagues, and anyone else you trust.

Estate planning may not be on the top of every business owner's mind, but something even more surprising happens when business owners look to raise money.

RAISING MONEY? PREPARE TO BE BOUGHT OUT.

Many startups think they need to raise money to grow their business. Sometimes that is true, but not always. Think about what that money will do for your business before committing to venture capital.

According to one of my trusted colleagues, in Canada, the average terms of a venture capital transaction are around $500,000 for a 20 percent stake in the business. In the US, a typical ask is $2 million for 20 percent. Therefore, raising money seems much more financially beneficial in the US than in Canada. In either case, however, there are hidden costs.

Raising money means you're diluting your own impact on the business. You're exchanging financial resources for a seat at the table. For some people, this works. Some business owners have been putting their own money into the business forever and need a boost to get ahead. Others might seek an influx of capital to invest in game-changing technology that will put them at the forefront of their industry. Still others might need money to pursue renovations they have been putting off for years due to a lack of liquidity.

Plenty of sound reasons exist to seek venture capital. However, if you go this route, be prepared to get an offer to buy you out. If a venture capitalist sees a business with the potential for a lot of growth, they won't let the opportunity pass. They'll contact you about an offer for more than just a minority stake. If that happens, make sure you're not caught off guard. Call your most trusted advisor and discuss what action to take next.

Capital raises often turn into M&A. This notion was universally agreed upon by the professionals I spoke with. In this situation, the owner often agrees to give up the majority share of their business for a dollar amount that blows them away. Usually the owner will stay on for a while as a consultant. For many people, this works out great because it allows them to move on. However, you need to ask yourself if this is what you really want. Are you ready to walk away from your business? What will you do when you're no longer needed in that consulting role? As is often the case, personal considerations might outweigh the financial benefits.

If you determine that selling is the right move after getting an offer to buy you out, be ready for anything. From my experience, 80 percent of these acquisitions fail for various reasons. Sometimes, there's a culture clash between the new owners and management. Other times, the founder ends up at odds with the buyer because they can't reconcile the books or negotiate a fair deal.

Treat a buy-out as you would any other exit strategy. You want professionals working for you on the accounting, wealth advisory, and legal sides.

The buyer may want to accelerate the process, but everything is negotiable. Don't agree to anything that makes you feel uneasy and trust the advice of your valued team members. In the end, you could end up with a highly lucrative deal, but beware of any potential pitfalls before handing over the keys.

EXIT STRATEGY TAKEAWAYS:

- Whatever your situation as a business owner is, there is one cardinal rule to remember about exit planning: the sooner, the better.
- A good corporate structure and clean books are essential to getting your business sold in a timely manner and for top dollar.
- Tax planning.
- Take time to consider proper estate planning. Consult with your attorney and have the terms of where your funds go in the event of something unexpected and unfortunate like bankruptcy, divorce, death, etc.
- Raising money is well-suited for some business owners, but not all. Think carefully before seeking venture capital and prepare to be bought out if/when you do.

BUSINESS OWNERS TELL THEIR EXIT STRATEGY STORIES

Understandably, the information you've collected to this point is a lot to take in. Congratulations on your initial education on exit strategy. My best piece of advice is not to let any of the processes mentioned scare you.

As a wealth advisor, I've been a part of many successful exit strategy teams for various clients. To date, the only difference I have seen is the degree of success. No deal I've been part of or heard of has gone drastically wrong. In the worst-case scenario, some money was left on the table. Even in those situations, the owner was still able to walk away with enough wealth to live beyond comfortably, continue to give to their most cherished charities, and leave a lucrative legacy behind.

Exit strategy isn't about triumph or tragedy; it's more about how much you gain, financially and personally.

I'd like to share some of the most impactful personal anecdotes from business owners who have already gone through the sale process. This collection includes both ends of the success spectrum. In one case, the business owner didn't get quite as much money as they could have for their business. In another case, the business owner walked away with no regrets.

Although the names, facts, and figures have been altered for anonymity, the lessons learned provide critical information about how exit strategy—good and not quite as good—works in the real world. This book is not meant to be a textbook with a lot of raw data, but it is intended to help you understand how to think about your own exit strategy.

LOST OPPORTUNITY

We'll start with an exit strategy story that didn't go as smoothly as yours will. You've gathered plenty of good information to know how to plan for an optimal result. Keep in mind, he still sold his business for plenty of money. He just didn't get as much value as he could have from the sale.

Kyle was the owner of a business that had been in the family for a long time. It had been handed down from his father, but a few years ago, the time was right to sell. Kyle had plans to reinvest the profits into another venture that was going to continue the family legacy as successful entrepreneurs.

The problem was that Kyle didn't get great advice from his advisor. Whether fees were a concern or another reason was in play, Kyle decided to work with a smaller firm to handle most of the exit strategy.

As is the case with many family-owned businesses, nobody had an eye focused on the documentation. The books were a mess and the structure was poor. The right advice would have probably steered Kyle toward cleaning up those risks before soliciting offers. Instead, the smaller firm sought bids before attending to the proper house cleaning issues. What likely happened was that the smaller firm was in over its head and didn't have a solid plan for getting the business in order first.

Kyle expected to sell his business for $20 million but sold for just $14 million instead. He needed a more experienced firm to step in, realize that the books and the structure would take some time to clean up, and manage Kyle's expectations accordingly. That way, they could have at least presented him with the option of selling quickly for less money or taking their time to get a higher purchase price.

Once again, was this a tragic result? No. Kyle was still able to walk away and start another venture, one that is doing quite well. However, he didn't sell for what he expected or what the value would have been if the exit strategy had been executed properly. The result was less money for that next venture and probably a financial challenge or two that he could have avoided.

A CASE STUDY IN INCENTIVE BIAS

Incentive bias is a strong source of seriously conflicting interests. When it's not recognized, it can turn deals upside down. In those cases, the team member gets inordinately more value (for their time invested) from the deal than the owner.

Dave was a successful business owner who had just turned fifty. He had owned his business for more than two decades and had put every penny he could back into it. Finally, he decided that he wanted to take some of his investment out so he could enjoy a higher quality of life. He had more than earned it.

As every business owner can attest, Dave was extremely busy managing his day-to-day operations. So he had little time to find someone who would be willing to buy a minority percentage of his business. That was his way of cashing out a little. So he signed an engagement agreement with a sell-side advisor and made it clear that he was not seeking anyone who would be interested in having a majority stake. He wanted a minority partner only.

Dave's situation is a different exit strategy from what we've mostly been talking about. Dave didn't want to walk away from his business. He just wanted someone to invest in it. His advisor kept bringing in private equity firms who wanted either a majority interest in the company or a board seat. *Lesson to be learned: private equity firms will not buy into your business without taking control.*

It turns out that Dave's advisor had a big incentive bias to get the deal done. This may not seem like the worst thing. Everybody wants to get the deal done—but at what cost? Dave clearly laid out his terms to the advisor. He wasn't ready to retire, and he didn't want to hand over too much power.

Unfortunately, the advisor's network simply didn't have anyone interested in a minority stake in Dave's business. Rather than being upfront with Dave about the situation, the advisor allowed their incentive bias to waste everyone's time and possibly provide Dave with an outcome he never wanted. The advisor presented Dave with multiple opportunities to sell a majority stake in his business, but nothing aligned with what Dave had told him.

Eventually Dave cut ties with the advisor and reached out to his own network to find a suitable buyer for his business. Based on this result, Dave recommends investing in your network, because that may be where your buyer comes from. Examining your own network might be the first place to seek a buyer. Why pay an advisor or anyone else to find a buyer for you if you can simply bring someone in from some of your most trusted relationships?

In the end, Dave was forced to sell 70 percent of his business when he wanted to sell only 30 percent. He did not maintain a majority stake, but he did maintain peace of mind in knowing that the business was in good hands because he sold to someone he knew who was already working in the industry.

YOU GET WHAT YOU PAY FOR

Remember the cardinal rule of selling your business that I mentioned earlier: the sooner, the better?

Jim and Perry are two business owners who had the foresight to think about how they were going to exit their business twelve years before it actually happened.

Jim and Perry had no kids involved in their business, so they knew—in advance—that there would be no legacy manoeuvre to hand off the business to a family member. They didn't want to simply sell off the company one day to the highest bidder with no regard for their workers or the longevity of the business. Rather, both owners took action early on (twelve years ahead of time) to ensure a smooth transition of power. To prepare for this, they onboarded two younger partners, Robin and Peter, and devised a plan to increase their ownership stake in stages.

Stage one handed 10 percent of the business to the new partners at a discounted price. The initial thought was that they would increase this amount of ownership incrementally until the new owners could buy them out completely. Shortly after, the second stage of the plan transitioned another 10 percent of the company to the younger partners, giving Robin and Peter a total of 20 percent stake in the business. This division of ownership remained in place for several years. During this timeframe, the business became exponentially more successful, and the four owners worked out an agreement where Jim and Perry became chairmen of the board, and Robin and Peter became president and vice president.

Eventually Robin and Peter wanted to sell the company to an outside buyer, rather than pay off the original owners for many years. Subsequently, they spoke to their auditors. They had a division that dealt with M&A and could determine a business valuation and work on a pitch on how the division would sell the company for them.

After getting the pitch from their M&A division, all four owners decided to explore alternatives, just to perform due diligence and ensure they were getting all the information needed from various sources to maximize the value of their sale. Jim contacted a former partner at his old CPA firm who worked in the M&A division of one of the "Big Four" accounting firms.

The firm did a lot of homework. They thoroughly investigated the business, its marketplace, and the industry. It was an impressive presentation that struck all four owners in a positive way. They figured that being aligned with such a big name would add value in the eyes of potential buyers. After careful consideration, the owners knew the big accounting firm was the right choice to sell their business and awarded them the bid.

After securing the job to sell the business, the firm quickly got to work. A team was assigned to help the business owners solicit high-quality buyers. They gathered information on other businesses in the same industry that might be looking to make an acquisition. The team also put together a presentation and distributed it to whoever might be a good fit as a buyer.

A few responses came forth; one of them was a division of a large Japanese organization with a presence in Canada and the US. Mainly, this company was hoping to shore up a larger market share in Canada.

The Japanese company began negotiations with the firm on the owners' behalf. A mutual interest became clear, but as offers were exchanged, an obstacle proved immovable. At the time, an auto pact existed with the US and Canada, and the deal fell through.

All was not lost after the derailed deal with the Japanese company. Because the owners went with a reputable firm they vetted for themselves, their exit strategy team quickly went back to work, reintroduced the potential sale to the marketplace, found a new buyer, negotiated all the terms, and closed the deal within a two-year timeframe.

In this particular case study, we see the value in hiring a team of professionals with expertise to perform all the phases of an exit strategy. The four owners got assistance in many areas they may have struggled with if they attempted to execute the deal in-house or with a smaller, less expensive M&A firm. For example, the company had only one major product line and one major customer that accounted for an inordinately high percentage of sales in some years. There was a common concern that many high-quality buyers would become disinterested from that fact. Team members from the big accounting firm worked with the supplier and the customer and discovered that the founders were transitioning the business to junior owners, who were staying on, meaning business relationships would be unaffected for the foreseeable future.

When asked about the most important aspect of a business sale, all four owners said: "Don't let fees sway your decision. You get what you pay for."

SELL, SELL, SELL: THE MOTIVATION OF A SERIAL ENTREPRENEUR

Some business owners love the startup phase. They're excited to create something new and get it off the ground. However, after things get up and running, they have no desire to think about managing day-to-day operations. Serial entrepreneurs want to innovate and change the world, but they don't always want to stick around to manage the business long term.

Neil is a brilliant serial entrepreneur whom I know. His idea is to incubate, scale, and sell within five years. That process has worked so well for Neil; he has done it three times. Who knows how many more will follow? If this sounds like something you'd like to do, Neil has offered some advice.

First, he explains that most buyers don't want the founder to hang around after a sale. Sometimes a buyer will ask the seller to stick around on a consultative basis for six months or so, but eventually the buyer wants to put their own stamp on the business. This is one way M&A can occasionally lead to culture clash. If the founder sticks around too long, they may develop an alliance within the company.

If that happens, there could be two opposing forces within the company even after the founder leaves. It's easy enough to avoid this, however. Come to terms about how long the founder will provide consultation and stick with it.

One thing I found particularly interesting that Neil had to say was to expect negotiations to fall apart eight to ten times before the deal closes. "Everybody wants everything, and nobody wants to pay for any of it," he told me. Both sides, however, should understand the importance of never burning a bridge in business. The last thing the buyer wants is for the seller to become a problem after the sale. Similarly, the seller doesn't want to waste their time doing that. It behooves both parties to act in good faith, have comfortable exchanges, and move the process forward until the deal is done.

THINK ABOUT YOUR LIFE PLAN

Another business owner I spoke with, Greg, told me a little about his recommendations to others looking to sell their business. He advised anybody to be aware of their post-exit lifestyle. Greg cautioned that most people think about how much money they can cash out for, but don't give enough consideration to what they'll do after they sell their business.

Most business owners are great at running, building, and operating their business, but they need to approach retirement with the same dedication. Post-sale, they'll need to focus on integrating their relationships, family needs, and social interactions. That's not as easy as it sounds for someone who may have worked twelve-hour days for the last thirty years or more.

You'll likely need a life plan after your exit plan. If you're thinking about operating another business, then your next plan is pretty much settled. Continue enjoying your life as a serial entrepreneur and best of luck in changing the world! If, however, you're actually retiring from the business world, you need to think about what you want to do next.

It's not enough to just think you'll walk the dog a few times a day and spend more time with the grandkids. Think about how you'll become emotionally fulfilled. Will you travel? Do volunteer work? Join a book club? Start a new exercise routine? Take up ballroom dancing? What about painting or music? There are plenty of options to live life to the fullest. Think about what you like to do and go for it. Even if you think you like cooking but realize after burning your first beef Wellington that you don't like it...move on to the next thing. Maybe baking is your thing?

If you know other business owners who have retired, ask them about how they've adapted to their post-business lives. The only thing that doesn't work in this situation is retiring to the couch. You'll be surprised at how quickly that can lead to a lack of purpose. Find activities that you can do every day and make the most of your post-business life.

AN EXIT STRATEGY WITH NO REGRETS

In my personal experience, I've seen a lot of exit strategy success stories. One comes to mind, in particular, involving a business owner from central Canada who sold his business at top dollar. Want to know how he did it? He had exceptional planning.

This individual personifies a rags to riches story. Brian was a super smart kid who came from almost nothing. In his mid-twenties, he moved to a big city and began earning a much higher than average income while working for a corporation.

Like many of us at that age, success can lead to trouble. Brian got caught up in a high-flying lifestyle. Not many twenty-three-year-olds are emotionally equipped to make great decisions regarding financial abundance.

Substance abuse became a big problem for Brian. It ended up causing a dismissal from his corporate job, even though he was tremendously talented at his role. As is often the case, there was a silver lining to that harsh outcome. The reality of losing his job caused him to reflect on his life, and he vowed to claw his way back toward success while never making the same mistakes again.

Soon after his fall, a colleague reached out to Brian and helped him turn his life around. He got sober and stayed that way. At the same time, Brian realized that one of the reasons he turned to drugs and alcohol was a lack of purpose in his life. Working for someone else didn't provide him with any career satisfaction.

To pursue that sense of purpose, Brian opened his own business and found tremendous personal value in the relationships he developed with his clients. He enjoyed working with them to change their lives for the better. Brian had found a deeply fulfilling and satisfying career.

Thirty years later, Brian had reached a level of success in his business and personal life he had never expected; he got married and had two sons, one of whom he brought into the business. Meanwhile, his business became worth millions of dollars.

From day one, Brian had set up his business to be ready for a sale someday. Again, not everybody is capable of doing this. If you're strapped for cash, as many startups and smaller businesses are in the early days, you may not be able to pay the fees upfront to initially structure your business so soundly. If possible, however, getting off on the right foot will make things immeasurably easier and more profitable in the end. It certainly was in this case.

Brian had all the right professionals in place from the beginning. He had a trusted CPA, a sharp attorney, and a talented business valuator with whom he formed a strategic partnership. Brian also incorporated his business, established clean books (and kept them that way), and set up trusts for his kids. Furthermore, he updated the structure of the business every few years to make sure the valuation was in-line with his expectations. This also allowed him to ensure he would have a favorable tax treatment while running his business and when looking to sell.

During his ownership, Brian grew the business at a prosperous rate of around 15 percent every year. Smartly, he didn't make the mistake of standing still while watching his money grow. Brian always maintained solid relationships with his colleagues and other industry insiders. He never burned a bridge. Simultaneously, he mentored staff, ensuring that operations would continue seamlessly in the event of his departure.

Sadly, one of Brian's sons passed away in his mid-twenties. This caused Brian to take another introspective look at his life. He was fifty-eight years old when this happened and decided it was time to walk away from his business to maintain a deeper level of appreciation for what he had in his life.

Because he had thought of his exit strategy in the beginning, Brian was able to sell for top dollar. He was paid 70 percent upfront for a large transaction price. He was also able to hand out significant bonuses to the staff members who had worked so hard for him over the years and supported him professionally and personally in his most challenging times.

Brian exemplifies what it's like to set up a successful exit strategy. Some of the most crucial aspects happen behind the scenes. Because he built and maintained positive relationships throughout his ownership, the owner of his primary office location approached him with an attractive offer. They had established a pleasant working relationship for many years, so there were no stressful negotiations happening back and forth. Instead, Brian received a more than fair offer with the best possible tax structure surrounding the deal. He also had the proper money allocated for estate planning, tax planning, insurance, and a life plan with which he could move forward.

That life plan has allowed Brian to split his time between a rural town just outside of Toronto and a family home in Arizona.

He enjoys playing guitar, hiking, and other outdoor activities, and now he has plenty of time for all of those, as well as more time to spend with his wife, son, and grandchildren. He also manages quite a bit of traveling.

As for the son he brought into the business, he is still working there today. Thanks to Brian's mentorship, his son is doing quite well and owns a portion of the business.

Brian implemented his exit strategy with no regrets. He got everything he wanted out of the transaction financially and personally. The thing that separates his plan from other less successful exit strategies is how well-organized he was.

This story encapsulates many (if not all) of the lessons explained throughout this book. Plan early, keep your books clean, build good relationships, think about taxes, hire a solid exit strategy team, and sell when the time is right (from both a market perspective and a personal one).

THIS RECIPE FOR SUCCESS DOESN'T CHANGE

Now, what about that business you've spent years—or even decades—building from humble beginnings to a profitable and prominent presence?

With all the information you've gathered, ask yourself the same question that began this book: "Is it time to sell?"

In the Introduction, I said that if the answer to that question was yes, you had come to the right place. At this point, you've learned a lot about exit strategy. If you are still ready to sell, you have a good idea of what you need to do, how long you need to do it, and who to talk to.

If you've decided that you're not ready to sell yet, keep this book handy as a reference tool. Most of the lessons learned will be just as relevant many years from now, and they can set you up for success when your time does come. Proper planning, managing expectations, having good people in place doing what they do best will always be a recipe for success.

EXIT STRATEGY TAKEAWAYS:

- Don't become overwhelmed by the planning involved with an exit strategy. The worst-case scenario is usually that the owner makes a substantial profit but doesn't get top dollar.

- Buyers want minimal risk. Look into any possible action that can take the risk out for your buyer. At the least, you'll want to de-risk your business by normalizing the earnings in your books and ensuring competent management is in place for the post-sale transition.

- Different business owners sell for different reasons. The timing of the market or your personal life may be just right. If both are in place, even better!

- Thinking about what you'll do after you sell the business is equally as important as getting top dollar. If you're selling because you have another venture ready to begin, great! If you're planning on retiring, think of a good life plan. Consider if you want to travel, exercise, spend more time with family, take part in hobbies, and other activities. It's likely that your sale has provided you with the opportunity to enjoy a life free of career commitments. Enjoy it!

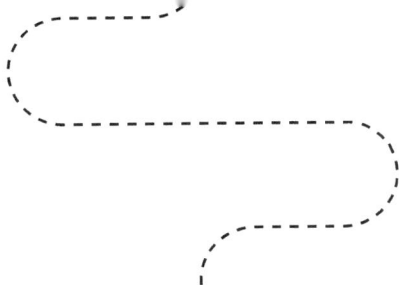

CONCLUSION

The moment of truth has arrived! Are you ready to implement your exit strategy? As you know, even if you're not prepared to sell, that doesn't mean you shouldn't start planning for the day you want to leave.

The next thing you should do is get educated about your unique plan for an exit strategy. Start by understanding what your business is worth. Then build a team of professionals around you to prepare the company to be worth its optimal value.

If you already have a trusted CPA, wealth advisor, and accountant, ask yourself if they're still equipped to handle the sale. If you discover that one or more of your team members is not ideally suited for the size of your potential transaction, begin the process of recruiting, hiring, and training someone else to get them up to speed.

Once your team is in place, they should collaborate on all the things that need to happen for your business to sell at top dollar...whenever that might be.

Here's a checklist of things to remember when forming your exit strategy:

- Exit strategy is all about preparedness. Start five years in advance.
- Consider your situation in life, as well as financial matters.
- Take the perspective of a potential buyer. What would you look for?
- Ensure a strong management team is in place.
- Have well-defined policies and revenue-generating processes.
- Reliable and verifiable accounting data is critical running up to the time of sale.
- Secure any goodwill in the relationships you've fostered over the years with customers and employees that can be transitioned to the new owner.

- Be able to show a consistent history of timely reporting and filings.
- Maintain compliance with regulatory and industry standards.
- Structure early.
- Make it easy for the buyer to confirm value by cleaning up messy balance sheets. Remove redundant assets, pay out shareholder advances, and satisfy liabilities not directly related to operations.
- **When considering a sale to children/family:**
  - Ask yourself honestly, "Can they do it? Are they active in the business? Do they have the skills and aptitude to successfully run it?" Have a discussion with your chosen family successor.
  - Do I need to balance assets to the other children? What is fair, or should everything be divided equally? Consider the time, effort, commitment to run the business vs. passive assets distributed to children not involved.
  - How is a transfer to a child financed? Many ways are possible. Consider bank financing. You may need to provide some financing by a vendor take back loan or alternative structure. Seek your current bank first as they

know your business. You can also create a new entity that is sold to obtain the capital gains exemption (CGE).

○ Even when selling to a family member (or especially when doing so), you need to remember to ask, "How do you get your money?"

- When selling to employees:
  ○ Similarly to children, ask yourself, "Are they capable of running the business?"
  ○ How will they secure financing?
  ○ You could devise a plan to increase their responsibilities for the business over time and intro into ownership positions.
  ○ When do you bring them in and how? Consider stock options, employee ownership trust, Employee Stock Option Program (class that means ownership).
  ○ Providing tax efficiency for employees is critical.
  ○ Determine the characteristics of the ownership interest to be issued. Include an audited financial statement. Make sure you use tight agreements.
- When seeking a third-party buyer:
  ○ Considered an "arm's length" sale, meaning

neither party directly communicates with each other throughout most of the process.

- ◦ Search your own network first for potential buyers.
- ◦ When hiring an outside firm to seek potential buyers, be especially aware of any incentive bias that may not serve your best interests.

- Much of the sale process can be broken down into three considerations, which are taxes, accounting, and legal:
  - ◦ **Taxes:**
    - ▪ Evaluate tax efficiency of the proposed transaction. Always ask yourself and your trusted advisor, "Is there a better way?"
    - ▪ Hybrid, asset, share; cost basis step-up; purification for CGE.
    - ▪ Qualifying Earn Out, Subsequent personal planning; LCGE (lifetime capital gains exemption) planning; purchase price allocations.
    - ▪ Cross-border tax issues; may have further tax deferral; can lose CCPC (Canadian-controlled private corporation) status; planning opportunities.

- **Accounting:**
  - Ensure financial statements are up-to-date and reflect accurately the underlying financial fundamentals.
  - There are working capital considerations such as change of control prior to sale/succession.
  - Ensure redundant assets have been addressed (presale transaction).
  - Leave working capital in books for an increased purchase price.
- **Legal:**
  - Build your team with qualified advisors and lawyers who have expertise in the correct area.
  - Ensure seamless communication between all team members to protect yourself against legal action and ensure the best result in your sale.

If the time is right, start recruiting your exit strategy team today. Even if you don't sell for thirty years, you'll be glad you started early.

ACKNOWLEDGEMENTS

Writing this book was incredibly enjoyable because of all the wonderful people willing to help me put these words to paper.

I must begin by thanking my mother, Ellie, whose constant feedback and support from a lifetime of journalism were instrumental to the completion of this work.

Thank you to all my business owner friends, especially: Dave, Stephen, Greg, Scott, Neil, and Brett. Your stories and openness were irreplaceable.

These pages would still be incomplete without the additional assistance from the many professionals who serve clients as well as I do: Ryan Baulke, Aaron

Rumley, Ali Spinner, Paul McVean, Mario Maruzzo, Brandon Lewis, Evan Marcus, and Chris Thomson.

My sincere gratitude also goes out to my publishing team at Scribe Media, especially David Caissie for the many hours spent working through ideas with me and helping to bring my words to life.

Finally, thank you to Sam Martin and his mother, Bronwyn, for helping me to clarify several critical ideas.

ABOUT THE AUTHOR

ALEX CARTER is the branch owner of multiple Assante Capital Management Ltd. locations. Since taking over his father's branch in 2011, he has grown the business to five times the value of what he originally paid for it.

As a senior wealth advisor to high net worth families, Alex enjoys the collaborative process of working with people to accomplish their goals in life and legacy.

Alex has qualified for Assante's Chairman's Council and Chairman's Council Elite program—a program recognizing the firm's top advisory practices—every year since becoming an advisor in 2007. He was also the recipient of Assante's Top 40 Under 40 award for 2019 at Assante's National Advisor Conference, awarded to the top overall ranking of advisors under 40.

In addition to being the branch owner, Alex is also qualified to serve as a Certified Financial Planner (CFP), Chartered Investment Manager (CIM), and Certified Executive Advisor (CEA), among many other esteemed industry distinctions.

Before his financial planning career, Alex attended Western University in London, Ontario. Not only did he achieve the Dean's list every semester, but he was also captain of the squash team that went undefeated in Canada and reached the Top Eight in First Division NCAA for four years. He remains a highly competitive international squash player today.

Additionally, Alex and his father have founded and maintained philanthropic foundations to assist the disadvantaged and provide for the greater good. Giving back is a big part of the humanity that Alex displays as a professional.

Today, Alex has homes in Toronto and Collingwood, Ontario, where he enjoys spending time with his wife and children. Alex is also enthusiastic about travelling, outdoor activities, and, of course, playing squash.